GOD OF

GOD

OF

SHADOWS

LORNA CROZIER

 McCLELLAND & STEWART

Library and Archives Canada Cataloguing in Publication
is available upon request

ISBN: 978-0-7710-7313-7
ebook ISBN: 978-0-7710-7314-4

Cover design by Jennifer Lum

Typeset in Dante by M&S, Toronto
Printed and bound in Canada

McClelland & Stewart,
a division of Penguin Random House Canada Limited,
a Penguin Random House Company

www.penguinrandomhouse.ca

1 2 3 4 5 22 21 20 19 18

Penguin
Random House
McCLELLAND & STEWART

All these words, these gods, are for Patrick.

CONTENTS

BOOK II

BOOK III

*"Whatever is fickle, freckled (who knows how?)
With swift, slow; sweet, sour; adazzle, dim;"*

GERARD MANLEY HOPKINS, "PIED BEAUTY"

"Whether or not they exist, we're slaves to the gods."

FERNANDO PESSOA

*"When I saw the dark clouds, I wept, Oh Dark One,
I wept at the dark clouds."*

MIRABAI, "THE CLOUDS"

PROLOGUE: AND GOD SAID

Who is the god who utters you? Is it the lame god who drags his foot down the road and the dust rises, fills your lungs, and makes you blind?

Is it the god who runs her tongue over the morning, and you smell her breath

like horse-chewed fescue, except it's not that smell. It's the scent of yourself on your fingers

after you scratch your head, the whiff of hair and scalp and your clearest thinking.

Most days, it's surely the god of the mind who utters you. The heart and gut are another affair.

You want to hear them too, their syllables of blood and fecal matter, but that needs more of you than you can give right now

and any god can only say so much. Whichever one, her own name is what she utters when she utters you. His own name

is what he utters when he pushes you from his nothing-womb into the ruinous noun-thick world.

BOOK I

"The gods are fugitive guests of literature.
They cross it with the trail of their names
and are soon gone."

ROBERTO CALASSO

God of ARITHMETIC

Most children no longer know who this god is. For one thing, he uses chalk as if time does everything but erase. In abandoned country schools, he prints columns of numbers on the blackboards. There are no pupils to add them up and call out the answers though his pockets burn with stars to give away. His worshippers, in danger of dying out, recite the time tables like Hail Marys under their breath to prove their minds are still okay. No matter what they've lost—the word *geranium*, the birthdates of their children—they can do their sums. He wanted his only commandment to be included on the tablets Moses brought down from the mountain, but the others, bartering for space, thought it was only about arithmetic and left it out. It would have changed the world. It would have made us kinder. *Thou shalt carry the one,* he intones to the small desks in empty classrooms, *carry the one.*

God of MATTER

Resists abstractions. You throw them at her, *justice, equilibrium, shame,* and she bats them back. Try *comely,* try *ugly,* they're of no concern. She puts her stick into any matter, into anything that matters, and gives it a stir. Then she asks the most important question: Does it need more salt? When she sees *worry* on a page she rubs it out and writes in *toe.* She writes *snout* over *soul; pine cone* over *ego; a thousand grains of sand* over *sorrow.* No wonder she's the one you light a candle for in the tool shed, the root cellar, the attic full of many things. After much beseeching and your generous donations to the poor, she lets you write *hope,* though to temper it, you must intone under your breath one of the following: a. *the peeling skin of paint under the lid of the can;* b. *the wishbone drying on the windowsill;* c. *the line a shrew draws in the dust on the floor of the cabin with his needle nose.*

God of STONES

Don't underestimate their sagacity, even the stones you'd call dull. In steeples, in the walls of llama sheds and stupas, on gravel pathways, they've been meditating for quite some time. Really, all are philosopher's stones. *I think, I think, I think*, they declaim with gravitas. Inside each, even those that fit inside a pocket, are two rivers, a herd of floppy-eared goats, wisdom teeth, and a clock, its metabolism so slow you can't hear it ticking. Inside each, no matter what its mineral composition, are a dozen stars, a braid of hair, a padlock, and a holy writ you can't decipher. When you try to read it out loud, your tongue, momentarily, turns to stone.

God of GOODBYE

That simple word god has given you has goodness at its core. Moths come to your porch to dust you with goodbye; a black beetle trundles over gravel on his way to something new. You get down on your knees and stroke his back, lightly, so he won't stop. Every rain says *adieu* to the sky, snow waves a hundred handkerchiefs as it falls. When the crows left the ark no one knew they weren't coming back. Smoke never returns to wood. The raped girl says farewell to her body. She is no more than the faint sound of a cat lapping water though the cat she remembers is buried under the white peony tree in the garden. The long-distance runner with thunder clouds on his lungs shakes hands with the city before his legs propel him past the finish line. Even trainless towns have station platforms where the dead depart.

God of DOGS

She thought she was going to be the god of gods. Her disappointment, however, didn't last—her mortal flock ended up enchanting her. Their exuberance is like a tired fountain suddenly exploding with noisy water. She'll always be the youngest of the immortals—*Homo sapiens* have it wrong: don't multiply a pooch's age by seven, divide your own. Somewhere, while you're doing the math, a mountain dog is digging through a snowdrift to a muffled cry; a water dog is holding a child's head above the waves; a mutt is hanging on to the arm of a thug who tried to strike his master. Emily Dickinson wrote in a letter, "I hope you love dogs too. It's economical. It saves going to heaven." She actually said, "I hope you love birds too," but it could have been dogs, if she'd been less timid, less housebound, don't you agree?

God of FIRE

Ungendered, faceless, it lacks a proper name. The most ecstatic, the most evangelical, it converts the inhabitants of cardboard slums and castles, banks and butcher shops; every citizen—human, four-legged, webbed, and winged—baptized by flames. Moths in Mormon suits carry embers of devotion from stoop to spire, from the edge of the city to the trees and the grass. The god of fire springs, it rolls, it punches. Nothing bounds across a river so nimbly, so fast. Only snow can purify as radically, as far. Ash Wednesday, ash all the other days too. Scrupulous scholars, their mouths and noses masked, sift through the cinders, use soot mixed with spit for their ink. They've been sent by the School of Devastation. You catch glimpses of their writing on scrolls of flame that roll and unroll in the infernal wind.

Darwin described the mad proliferation of flowers in the Cretaceous period as "an abominable mystery." Abominable because the flowers blithely destroyed his notion that nature doesn't make a leap. The unknown perpetrator of his distress, which lasted until his death, was the god of sex. For almost 80 million years, she obsessed over the pistils' juicy tips, the nectar-loaded stamens. When she tired of her outrageous panoply of perfumes, forms, and colours available in every size, she bumped things up. She focused on one specific family, orchids, fine-tuning them until there were 30,000 kinds.

One bears such a creepy resemblance to a fly that horny flies buzz up and mount it. Another's musk mimics the scent of a female bee, inexactly, because bees thrill unabashedly when the smell's slightly off, when it's almost familiar, forbidden. If insects are in short supply, the Chinese orchid will twist 360 degrees and pollinate itself. When she brought to life the world's biggest flowerhead and doused it with the stink of corpses, the other gods called a halt, but not before she tweaked the titan arum so it could turn up its own heat to exaggerate its stench. The garden, once a paradise, filled with carrion beetles and carrion flies.

Fish were up next, and later humans, but really, flowers had devoured her imagination and her time. We got what we got, with little variation. Some say she let us down—our coupling's so appalling *that the human race would die out if lovers could see what they're doing.* Among this god's worshippers, those who see with rose-coloured lenses, one is already on her way to sainthood—a forty-five-year-old Japanese artist whose chosen name, Rokudenashiko, means "no-good-girl."

In a T-shirt and baseball cap, holding a paddle, she poses for a photo in a yellow fibreglass kayak shaped like her vulva. She made it from a silicone mould and a 3-D printer. Through watching videos from Canada's North, she's learned to perfect her stroke. As long as she stays on water and out of jail (twice she's been arrested), it's going to take her where she wants to go. To welcome her, the god of sex will be waiting on whatever shore, arms full of flowers.

God of FORGETTING

Is it a blessing or a scourge, forgetting? That's still up in the air, so much so there are two gods to ensure both arguments survive. Like a couple in a lasting, though sometimes wobbly marriage they're meant to help each other, for they, like their petitioners, forget. So many strings tied around their fingers they've taken to wearing macramé mittens. A timer, similar to the one you bought from the hardware store, hangs from a cord around each of their necks. The constant *tic-tic-tic* they can't escape is like an ant breaking sticks in their ears. When the alarm goes off, they may have lost track of what they were called on to help their supplicants remember. The baker's bread about to blacken in the oven and burn the shop down; the life jackets abandoned in the trunk of the car as the man pulls the cord on the motor and heads out into the waves with his son. Usually they're involved with less important tasks, igniting sparks in the dimness of the brain to remind you to save the ice cream you left on the car seat, to turn off the garden hose you got going the evening before. When your prayers remain unanswered, don't take their unresponsiveness to heart. Sometimes they apply the solutions meant for you to another person though they insist they don't forget a face. A woman unexpectedly blurts out what wasn't on the tip of her tongue but someone else's; a man recalls a lover he never had and sends her roses. Help these divinities if you can. Place a sticky note with your request where they'll likely see it, perhaps beside the sausage roll you left on the kitchen counter with the sign *Eat This*, in case they forget to eat.

God of NEXT-TO-NOTHING

She's an expert on exactness. In the left pan of the weigh scale, she puts next-to-nothing; in the opposite, an apostrophe, the front left leg of a midge, the millimetre mark on a wooden ruler. Even on its own, each is heavier than what she's been chosen to watch over. She finds the soul of thieves, the soul of meanness, the soul of envy. She puts them, scrawny and brittle, one by one, on the right. With each, she's surprised they still bear a burden—every time, there's a drop in their direction. Finally she finds the soul of a sleepwalker. Halfway to being something else, almost done with earthly things though it guides the body down the stairs, past the open wound of ditches and wells, this soul approaches the lightness she's been seeking. As she records her findings with a feather quill, the scale dips to one side then the other, surely on the verge of balance.

Birds eschew gods. They're all buddhas without the belly and the smile. Who needs a smile when you can sing? How much they can teach us. Like the heron who stands on one leg if he has one leg. Like the heron who stands on one leg if he has two. If you're bored, mimic the nuthatch who climbs the tree upside down.

In the North, ravens wait for wolves to rip the caribou carcass open. To kill time, they invent a new religion made entirely of sinews. Their feet are black because they wade into the darkness where sleep takes you every night. If you pay them enough attention, Zen-like, you may learn to leave your body and follow their three-toed footprints into no-form at all.

God of THE MOON

In spring it's a bowl of cherry blossoms as they open, a hint of rose turning white. You can also say it's a bowl of maggots: when they transmogrify into flies, the moon wanes. In times of hunger the moon's a plate of rice and fish. In fall it's a winnowing basket of ground corn, then a tortilla patted flat by a woman's hands. Sometimes, no matter what the season, there's blood in it. Is it a comfort to know the moon in the sky sees nothing? That's what keeps it distant and abstract. The moon's beauty is past change, though of course it changes. Praise it for its self-erasure, for its cool complacency. Praise it for its equal love of flies and blossoms, for its offer to mean. The winter moon is a whale's vertebra, turned on its side. Salt-pocked, sand-glistened. Can you say it's also what you see when you wear bones over your eyes in the snow so you won't go blind? Praise it for silence, for its patience with your blasphemy—the metaphors you lay on its altar like fattened living beasts.

God of NOSES

O, the marvel of her designs! The six olfactory organs on the ant's antennae; the mandrill's crimson proboscis, the same colour as his ass; the hound's nose that is smarter than most eyes.

Yet some of her cronies make fun of her. They're in charge of migration, black holes and quasars, the fate of the first-born child. One of them dares to laugh but suddenly he feels his own nose widen horrifically across his face. Then it dangles like a rubber hose he has to catch before it smacks the pearly floor.

Human beings irk her too. Think of the millions of nose jobs. And though people are willing to believe in almost anything, they don't believe in her. She zaps them with curses. Their noses burn and blister, grow blackheads and pimples, plug up with gobs of snot. In the most inappropriate of settings— a job interview, a formal dinner, a first date in a movie theatre before the lights go out—someone's index finger goes berserk (she's behind this), dives into his nostril, and picks and picks.

God of LAST RESORT

If you had the eye for it, you'd see her footprints glowing like phosphorous on the rails of bridges and around a solitary tree with an angled branch that could hold a body on a rope. Then there are kitchen ovens, cars left running in garages, bathtubs, tenth-floor windows. If it's someone's second try, she might not bother. Notice, she says, when they upbraid her, *last resort* is singular.

She shows up for the ones who keep on going, though she's weary of the notes they take so long to write and toss away. They call upon her from the daylight gloom of their sour beds. Sometimes there's a child standing in the doorway, afraid to enter. He holds the tray his mother uses when *he's* the one who's sick. There's an egg upon it and a slice of buttered bread.

Those who need her most can carry on for years. By the time she arrives, they've been whittled down or are so bloated with loss that when she touches them, the indents of her fingertips remain. She's been called many things, often in anger, but that's okay. The worst is the battlefields, the ruins of the cities. Soon she'll have to ask for leave—she knows the signs: her left eye is twitching and she can't lift her arms above her head.

Right now she is sitting on the blown ground of a farmyard, holding the head of a dead horse in her lap. To escape the soldiers, a boy has slit its belly and, with his little brother, crawled inside. Flies, usually leery of her scent of immortality, have lost their fear. They swarm from the horse's torn flesh and settle in her hair. They bead her eyes and lower lip. If she calls out, who will hear her? Who will bend from the clouds and lift her from this place, her skin crazed with smoke and ash, the places on her face where she still shines washed with tears?

God of WIND

Lean, this god, and empty.

No one has seen it, as the poet says.

Even in the heavens, it can't sit still, it remains invisible to the rest of the pantheon, yet it moves more gracefully and swiftly than the ones with wings. This creates much envy.

It doesn't like to find itself inside walls, even those that form a circle.

It lords over the four directions and the fifth direction that controls the heart. When it blows through you, your life's upended.

You think it comes from the mountains, the ocean? You think it comes from the west? Mistral, Papagayo, Santa Anna, Williwaw—the wind collapses anything you choose to call it.

Whither? is its favourite question. What it loves most on earth is an inky lung of starlings tossed into the sky. Of the human body, it loves hair.

God of CONTRARINESS

She spoons sand in the mouths of the emaciated, gives the weak of will five teenage daughters, the philosophers the answers they argue don't exist. As well as a breviary or two and the periodic table. She entices the incurable babbler—it is her nature—to buy property, sight unseen, in the City of Silence. He won't be able to flip it. She gives the child afraid of the dark a father who is only shadow. She makes the hunter of wild fowl deadly allergic to feathers. To the cynic she sends a baby in a basket, not necessarily a good baby, but a baby, nonetheless, when he expected a scorpion, a crock full of pebbles, a plastic shoe.

God of SLOW

The penitents ascend on their knees to the highest shrine, patellas worn thin as communion hosts. It takes more than a generation to reach the top. Children take over from their parents. What they search for is an answer. In their case, does *slow* mean *dim, thick*?

The dwarf trees on the peak conduct a sluggish wind. *How do you slow down time?* the seekers ask. Indiscernible to instruments of measure, toward the valley where people rush about, the mountain moves its granite thighs.

This, after all, is not the god of standing still.

God of HATEFUL THINGS

He has a hard time of it, as does his paraphernalia. Slugs, cockroaches, vats full of the muck that becomes wieners, bunions, and liver spots, the grimy carpet in the lobby of a cheap hotel. *What did I do to deserve this?* he asks, not expecting a reply. He himself is loved unconditionally by the others. They fill his pillow with lavender. They buy him freestone peaches. They lay out long, fat lines on Arborite and give him a crisp hundred-dollar bill. They let him shoot the farthest in the circle jerk. Meanwhile: tomato blight, the Out of Service sign on the last city bus, arch supports, blowflies, the dog slapping his tongue across your face after he's eaten a pile of human shit, on the beach a pile of human shit—oh, hateful, hateful things!

God of ACCEPTANCE

The landscape painter at the artist colony in the country noted for its messianic light, its sparse, hard-to-capture beauty, complains she's come all this way to paint *al fresco* but the mosquitoes have driven her inside, no matter the netting on her hat, her cuffed sleeves and pants, a heavy dose of Deet. They bite through everything. And when she tries to snap a picture, a breathy handkerchief of mosquitoes flutters over the lens. *What can I do?* she moans, trapped in a dull and narrow room, thinking of booking a ticket back to her studio in Vancouver. Paint the mosquitoes, god replies.

BOOK II

"Has All—
a codicil?"

EMILY DICKINSON

"Was God a metaphor, and if so, of what?"

STEPHEN DUNN

HER WORDS

(After Mahmoud Darwish)

When her words were sap
       she was bone;
when her words were water
       she was wren;
when her words were gravel
       she was sweat;
when her words were ashes
       she was heart—
           see, the moon is rusty,
the dust, weary—
when her words were mist
       she was the hands of lovers
that can't stop touching
       though they lie
in different pockets in the earth.

God of SHADOWS

Has a soft spot for twins. For blue hours of snow, for cumulus that drag their doubles across the ripening wheat, for Goths who wear nothing but black. Though he's without substance this god carries a lot of weight. Stretching out his arms across the sky, he can spread a shadow big enough to canopy a mid-size town, a city ghetto. To distract us from his less-than-sunny disposition, his partnership with death, he switches the setting from the darkened valley of Psalm 23 to a flat and treeless field where shade is cast only by the giant wheel of a tractor. Late August in that cool limbate circle, a man and woman unwrap sandwiches from a dish towel, open a tall red thermos, and eat and drink, a collie-cross who will be born again (same breed, same sex, same name) panting at their feet.

God of RENAMING

Her main job is to fix things up so you won't be nasty, to rechristen the creatures you work to wipe out. Slugs she yclepts *lawn dolphins;* gophers become *earth otters;* rats turn into *small-footed wayfarers of the dark.* The rats reject that: it could be almost anyone. Possums, raccoons, feral cats. She tries again, *Night's*—no; *Fear's*—no; *Fate's postal workers*: on an assembly line that sorts the mail, she can see rodent families decked out in standard blue-grey jackets. They'd stamp "Return" on any missives of doom Fate sends your way. To doubly ensure you'd never get the letters, others down the line eat the stamps and piss on the envelopes till the ink runs. Though she's pleased with this scenario, it's overly elaborate, too complex. Will it convince you of the rats' crucial role in your future happiness? Will it stop you from setting out the poison, the traps? The rats don't think so. And though they'd like the taste of glue, the nepotism, they hang on to *rat* with fierce rodent teeth.

God of QUIRKS: ITS MORE FAMOUS DEVOTEES

Emily Dickinson went in fear that strangers might see her handwriting. Her sister, therefore, addressed the envelopes of the letters Emily wrote. Miss Dickinson wore only white; so did Mark Twain, and his shirts, tailor-made, buttoned down the back.

A puzzled doctor noted that Malcolm Lowry's knuckles were callused like a chimpanzee's, who walks and runs on all fours. In Malcolm's case the hardened skin was caused by standing in front of a desk and leaning on his knuckles as he dictated his novels to his wife. If she wasn't with him while he was dressing for the day, he put on his shoes, then his socks.

On the promenades in the Jardin du Palais-Royal, Gérard de Nerval walked a lobster on a leash of blue ribbon. "Lobsters make the perfect pets," he said, "because they don't bark and know the secrets of the sea."

At the age of sixty-nine, to improve his sexual and creative vigour, William Butler Yeats travelled to Switzerland, where a doctor implanted monkey glands into his scrotum. One of his contemporaries on the board of the Abbey Theatre opined, "It's like putting the engine of a Cadillac into an old Ford."

Terrified of being buried alive, Hans Christian Andersen, with no attempt at humour, posted a sign by his bed: "I am not already dead."

Several residents of Walden Pond allege that Henry David Thoreau could swallow his nose.

De Nerval, who named his lobster Thibault, hanged himself when he was forty-six from a tall window grate in a Parisian alley, leaving only a brief note for his aunt: "Don't wait up for me this evening . . ." There's no formal record of what happened to Thibault, though a neighbour claims Gérard's aunt, ashamed to be seen on the streets with such a creature, kept it in shape by encouraging it to climb up and down the curtains. This she accomplished by placing its favourite snack, a pickled herring, on top of the wooden rod.

Yogi Berra voiced the wisdom of this, his favourite, god: "You can observe a lot just by watching."

She's the loveliest. Long white hair and the body of a retired prima ballerina, some severe Madam (fill in a name that sounds Russian) who teaches for meagre wages in the school where shoes bubble with blood. Her two renowned disciples, the dour brothers, went beyond her expectations: dozens of princes who starve to death in thickets, a fox with its head and feet chopped off, a dog deliberately crushed by a surly carter's wheels. It was not the Dog of History who, with his huge gloomy head and strings of drool, is her keen companion. He'd be less dangerous if he weren't so ugly and good-tempered. If he didn't grin when he sees you coming from the past. Oh, the horror, the horror, you can't help but say out loud. It's her favourite way for a bedtime story to end.

God of INSECTS

With a billion billion in his care, there's so much to consider that he gets help from the others (see the gods of noses, of sex, of astonishment, of bites).

There are insects he endowed with so much clout he may have gone too far: a tiny beetle can eat a pine forest, grasshoppers devour continents of wheat, termites chew until a town turns ghost. Some accuse him of gross egotism, of power-mongering. He defends himself by pointing out the delicacy of monarchs and mayflies, the ballet solo of the praying mantis, the song of field crickets, the dancing cartography of bees.

There's no shape he hasn't used—the thorn bug is a triangle, the kudzu bug's a square, and there's a treehopper that looks like a helicopter. He's dropped off members of this class on every inch of earth, inside the flesh and out, in palaces and hovels, in every climate. There are insects so cold-adapted, they'll die from the heat of your hand.

Most doctors of divinity agree he, of all the gods, has been around the longest and will outlast.

God of WATER

Her signs are willow wands and pitchers moulded from mud in the shape of shorebirds. She calleth forth water and she maketh it disappear. She knows the fountain of youth; she knows the dried well where the old ones gather and toss into its depths the dull coins of their given names. She bloodies the River Styx and gilds the mouth of the stream that flows through the gates of heaven. Mostly she's this colour: Aegean blue, Danube blue, Nile blue, South Saskatchewan blue, Pacific and Atlantic blue. None of them blue. That crow sent out to find dry land? It saw no end to water. It landed on her wrist as if it were Bedouin-trained, then went off again. Praise to her ears is the beat of its wings. And the *thou, thou, thou* hitting shingles and the tautness of tents, all around her the rivers running. That was the best of times, the undamned rivers running.

God of THINGS WITHOUT MERIT

There aren't many such things. Even bad TV might free a person from loneliness, the kind that maims. A red thingamajig with no purpose might, in the hands of a child, become a treasured toy. Can you accept one shoe for this category? Objects that have lost their other half? In the old days, one nylon stocking was used to replace a fan belt or tie a peony stem to a bamboo stake. One mitten carried a kitten to a vet. There's throwaway plastic, but it's too dangerous to drop off at the dump. This god is the ruler of junk stores: he transforms and mends, he miracles the worthless into objects of desire, that is, things that sell. Really he's doing himself out of a job. It's okay. He has hobbies. And in every country there will always be those who believe their whole lives fall with a clunk into this category: *without merit.* Even if they take care, without complaint, of an agèd parent, even if they own a chestnut mare who waits every morning for the barn door to open so she can look upon a beloved human face.

Like birds (neither appreciates the comparison) they don't need a god. They bring the light of their grace to the darkest of alleys, the darkest of times. They take to the air, to the trees, to the tallest highboy in the house, and look down at you with the gaze of a terrible deity. Unlike dogs they don't try to help out, that is, with the little things, with repeated tasks. They don't get upset at sirens. They can see the soul as it sloughs off the body, and if you're not ready, they bring it back or leave enough of it by your bed—a feather, a skinny tail, a transparent wing—to regenerate then slip inside the cage of your ribs.

God of BALCONIES

He can't help but think how expansive a balcony makes the meanest apartment! Like a substantial chin on an indifferent face, it juts and imposes a new personality. There's room for a bicycle, an old mattress, a hibachi, a potato plant, a fake tree with decorations, an aquarium, a surfboard, a hummingbird feeder, a red canoe. Only the railing draws a line. And the space it defines is the site of crucial happenings: the tryst that begins the affair while the spouses of the nascent lovers chat insipidly behind them in the well-lit room, a disgraced banker's leap to the cars below, the birth of five mice in a tumble of rags, the sliding of a paring knife across the smoothness of an arm. Moonlight comes to rest on the blade when the moon's had enough of rising.

God of THE DISREGARDED

There's a shine on the boy's belly where the mouth of this god kissed him. No one has kissed him there before. Only the wind fingers the old woman's hair (how she longs to be touched), opens her unbuttoned jacket. Because people in the city have stopped noticing the seasons, snow stops falling. Birds rattle the bushes so they'll be seen. A grey jay calls. On the way to the party the stench in the subway was so bad the couple held scarves over their mouths and nostrils until their stop at Bathurst. On the way home eight hours later— it was New Year's Eve, there was a crowd—they got in the same car. The heap of clothes that was a man still lay on the floor. God of the disregarded made the revellers, vigorously drunk and void of pity, step over, step over, in and out.

God of PUTTING-BACK-TOGETHER

When the man spackled the wall with his brains, did he think of his daughter, who had to clean it up, his wife, who had to force herself to eat from that day on? Yes, the gods are livid. They put him back together with duct tape, they used horn buttons for eyes, they gave him dandruff instead of hair, and a bad back. They put him under a bridge in a dying city where his wife and daughter would never see him. They tied his tongue, gave him a phobia for pigeons and the reek of sewers. Then they made him immortal. The gods of pity were too timid to interfere and besides, they'd been assigned another task, to comfort each snowflake in its long fall and its immaculate, gradual melt. They'd get to him when they had time.

God of ANONYMITY

When she decided to appear on earth, all the names and the need for names vanished. Given that, it's difficult to talk about what happened next. What was called *man, woman, gravel, grass* coexisted without distinction. *Stem, barbed wire, snail, oboe*. Energy flowed into the spaces that the nomenclature of type, class, and vocation used to occupy. The air was uncertain. She came down and walked you into the open. Blurring all distinctions, a breeze blew on everything at once. There was a nameless longing. What else? A bewilderment, a baffling consolation. It was as if the unsigned messages she sent had been written on the walls of some mother's womb, warmed by it, salted. In that state before mouth and mind shaped meaning, eye and ear (of fish, of canine, of aspen leaf?) were slowly opening; a vague heartbeat thrummed.

God of PUDDING

You knew there had to be one, didn't you? There are fewer kinds of pudding than species of beetle, but still enough flavours and textures that a divine fondness has to be behind it. What came first, the pudding or the spoon? That's this god's favourite ontological question. His buddies in the upper realms get a little tired of it, but there are more empyrean weaknesses than taste buds and this shortcoming is less annoying than most. Think of a pudding's special nature: you can eat this sweet before you have teeth and after you lose them. You can make a different variety every lunch and supper hour at a campfire or in a fancy kitchen in Dubai. And what could be more sacramental: one of the most delicious on the menu calls for day-old daily bread.

Okay, he's had trouble with PR. And with his design. He should've made bigger, cuter ears, as his sibling did with mice. He should've made a different tail. Even kept it the same but endowed with curly hair or uncurly hair, enough to hide the nakedness. Many claim the tail looks like a snake, to which, unfair to the snake, we seem to have a natural aversion. There's no resemblance, really, between rodents and reptiles. Herpetologists could tell you exactly why but an amateur knows too.

For one thing, the common garter snake is thicker than a rat's tail, more supple, beautifully green. And maybe, most importantly, snakes have a different nature. Unlike rats, they're shy. They don't want to hang around with us, they don't want to nest in our attics or piss in the insulation. We don't hear stories of them eating babies in New York. A snake is not a rat. A rat is a rat is a rat, Gertrude Stein might have said.

To our displeasure, their god gets them through the tiniest opening and endows their teeth with the ability to chew through the toughest matter: live electric cables between the studs, spark-plug wires in your car. So what if there aren't rat temples in your country? One running across the bedspread evokes more blasphemies and strikes more terror in the human heart than the god himself dropping from the sky on fiery wings.

God of THE NARROW-MINDED

Her task is to shock them into changing. To tuck a ferret in their trousers. To tangle a blackbird in their hair. To kiss with a scarlet mouth the endpapers of their sacred books. None of this works with the hard cases. They insist on the evils of immigration, the laziness of the poor, the rabidness of modern women, a.k.a, Fembos. There are tortures she can use—the convincing arguments of fire and fire ants, for instance—but that's not her style. She finds another way to ring their bells. When the front door opens, a bison bull crashes in, swinging his monstrous head full of thunder, breaking clocks and crockery, smashing couches, crushing walls. They flee their houses, they run through the night. Their north and south, their right and wrong, their *us* and *them* get muddled. Past the edge of town, in the darkness of the forest they denied was there, they stumble in ever-widening circles among the high thoughts of the trees.

God of BITES

One of the most powerful, most hard-working, he's got so much to watch over, to cause to occur. Think of that boxer and the torn-off ear, the soccer player turned vampire and banished from the game. Then there are pit bulls, along with the bred-to-be-more-gentle dogs maddened by chains, the feral cats you capture to get spayed, the mother crow who ripped a flap of skin off your neighbour's bald head. Not to mention the alligator, whose jaws can't be forced open unless it wants them to. As well, rose thorns and acacias, winter wind, nibbles of fear as you forget the names of things. Don't overlook the bugs, especially mosquitoes: this god has to be familiar with every single one. And then there's the snide remark and its reply, milk teeth on nipples, the teenager's chomp into her pillow to stifle her cries when she's fucking in her parents' basement. It all started with that first crunch in the Garden. Remember before the apple, the lion lay down with the lamb? Perhaps the lion licked the lamb's face, perhaps it wetly gummed the pink inside the woolly ears before this god bared his teeth.

God of THE MUTABLE

The most protean, the least likely to show up in a painting or become a graven image. Just when you think there's a form you can grab on to, this god shifts—animal, human; male, female, in-between. It's the holy ghost, kind of. Something like pure spirit but it's got an arm that rivals the best of pitchers'. When you want a straight answer, it throws that curve that flummoxed both Babe and Mickey. It smacks into the palm of your gloveless hand and hurts like hell. You never ask again. As for parables, good luck! All its stories begin the same way and no one's allowed to write them down: "We do not really mean, we do not really mean that what we are about to say is true." God of the mutable! Here's to you.

God of CLICHÉS

He's taken over the tattoo parlour. Draws valentines above the heart, butterflies on ankle bones. Writes MOTHER in curlicues on the tree planter's weary back, *LOVE* with roses across the businessman's bicep. In one week he carves a million tears. Even *he* gets tired. Snakes following the veins and JESUS SAVES. He'd like to cover the palest flesh from head to toe with a thousand needle pricks of snow. You'd have to get that close to see them and you'd feel the cold.

BOOK III

"From the Koran, from the Vedas and from
Deuteronomy,
From every dogma, full of fury, all the gods
Have come out into the open: Look out! and keep
a better watch."

PAUL VERLAINE

HIS WORDS

He was spit

when his words were apples,

he was grass

when his words were plows,

dog when his words were flies,

snow when his words were skulls,

he was melt

when his words

were written down.

Rot when his words

were iron. Given this,

think of all the things

he cannot say.

God of ASTONISHMENT

When Yahweh reveals himself to man, bushes burn, the mountains tremble, and the wings of his six-winged angels batter the air with thunder. The god of astonishment goes for a subtler theophany: the quiver of the rare bat that shows itself in daylight dipping into the pond then perching upright on the rafters of the tea house, spreading its wings to dry. The multitude of spider crabs that scatter in low tide, going sideways, as sore afraid as you to face what's ahead and what's behind; the common cockroach that if decapitated remains alive, its head still thinking; the jackrabbit jump of a woman's heart when she hears her husband of thirty years pull into the driveway in his red truck, its windows down, an old song on the radio, and then his words as the screen door slams: "I'm home." God speaks to us like that, in clear tones and not in riddles, yet sometimes we walk right through her on our way. When we do that, when we miss her brightness in the morning on Quonset roofs, in the yellow head of certain blackbirds, she's tempted to startle us in our tracks, to place her fiery mouth upon our mouths and fill our lungs with marigolds and bees.

God of THE DEAD

Needing a break from darkness, he takes his two-week vacations in high summer above the Arctic Circle. The rest of the year, he likes to nap in ICU rooms, all those harsh lights and alarms signifying a life about to end.

Where he rules there is a lack of active verbs; there is no present or future tense. Even nouns glance over their shoulders—they revert to what they were. *Daisy*, for instance, becomes an eye. Enough of them in a vase creeps you out. The beholder is beheld.

Yesterday he thought he heard someone singing badly over the waters. If it's another Orpheus, he must be told there's no looking back. Here everything is doubly lost, both then and then again. When this god listens to the dead breathing, what he hears is wind in the pages of a pageless book, wind in a clear-cut forest, wind in the hair of a woman whose head's been shorn.

God of BITTER

He puts the hard seed into the heart of the jawbreaker. Your mouth and tongue black, you bite into it and the taste of this god sweeps through you. You've known him all your life. He caused your father's acrimony to seep into the womb: he fed the cells that became your liver, lungs, eyes.

When you were born, your mother said, you had a sullen cry. The nurses gave you over quickly. Your father moved from job to job; the bosses niggardly, his co-workers—not as smart, he said—got ahead. Everything has a jaundiced cast to it as if you wear glasses smeared with ash from the weekly burnings at the nuisance grounds. Once, the caretaker there forgot to build a barrier fire around the perimeter and thousands of rats streamed into town. That made you smile.

You married the most adorable, most charming person you'd come across, she bore the dearest children, but it made things worse. You wanted to drown the stuffies, slash the tricycle tires, pinch the babies.

You keep thinking of your father's last expression, a grimace no undertaker could mask with wads of cotton and makeup pots. After the funeral when you walk through the door of your house, as usual your poodle, who loves your drunken mother-in-law more than you, won't stop barking and a puddle of pee spreads at your feet. You don't get rid of him. You're not mean, just hard-done-by. You'd stick your head into a hive of bees if you could do away with bitterness. You'd fight the biggest bear for the sweetness on his paws.

God of HORSES 1

Likes particularly to put them in a field at night, snow falling, and you don't know they're there. As you pause on your skis, you hear a tall exhalation, and when you look up, a horse stares right at you—sees you so clearly the stars stutter. Something higher than the horse—is it a ghost blanketed in snow, is it a pale rider?—bends toward you. *Cold* is the word made flesh, and far from any solace, you feel its grip around your chest. Strangely, you're not scared, but you can't cry out or walk away.

God of GUILT

So many, so many supplicants, they're close to needing a heaven of their own. A place of wallowing and muck. The groom who abandoned his high school sweetheart at the altar, the woman who gave up her sixteen-year-old cat so she could move into a luxury apartment, the man who drove his mother to the home and never went back—these are the worshippers though their faith is frangible and brief. They expect the gods to forgive them. Deep guilt, authentic guilt, belongs to the good of heart and spleen. What have they done? No one knows. They don't brag about their sins. They don't move on. If their souls could be scanned, the gods would see a luminous opacity, an accumulation like hoarfrost thickening on a windowpane, light struggling to shine through.

God of THE LEFT

Take it to the left, the jazz saxophonist said and his band knew
what to do. When you ask the loneliest customs agent in the
world on the border between Saskatchewan and Montana
how to get to the town your friend lives in, he says, *Stay on
this road. When you want to turn left, don't.* The bride behind
the wheel rabbited her car to the left and missed the church.
She lived happily on her own till her dress wore out. To deter-
mine who's in charge, once a month the god of the left
arm-wrestles her opposite. Sometimes she loses. For a few
days after her fist and forearm slam to the table—the wood
shattered—she has trouble holding a comb, a knife, a pen.
Easy to misread her handwriting and misinterpret what she
wants you to do.

God of DOUBT

Remember the parasite that thrived inside a man for twenty years without his knowing? Doubt's like that. Once it's been around for a while, even if diagnosed and treated, it won't go away. It doesn't stop you completely but you stumble and don't go far. It lacks the vigour of a total loss of faith, the punch in the face you feel when you catch your lover cheating. It's like an invisible puncture you notice in the inner tube only when you're in the middle of the lake and can't swim back. This god steps up once the book has been sent out for review, the painting's on the wall, the overly confident piano waits for you on stage. Doubt rinses you in its sullied water; you come out dripping but unborn again. You fall—not into St. John's dark night of the soul but into a prairie dusk stretched long and thin. Doubt's divinity hangs around like smoke blowing in from summer forest fires, a thousand miles north but changing all you see. Tinged with red, stricken, the sun's a slow ineffectual bleed.

In human years, she's eleven and will be that age forever. All she wants is horses. She runs with them in the meadow, curls beside them in the stalls, curries them until they gleam with her single-mindedness. Her incense smells of hay and horse dung. To amuse herself when she's bored at holy gatherings and can't just ride away, she chants under her breath: *Withers, fetlocks, dock, barrel, poll, throat latch.*

The first horse she created was no bigger than a fox. She carried it from continent to continent in a sack on her back. That felt demeaning to the horse. It grew larger. She debated with herself for centuries over the option of adding wings. Some of her cohorts advised it. But she wanted horses—their beautiful unfeathered ankles so strong and slim, their hooves drumming—to love the earth and never long to leave it, even though like us they cannot stay.

God of GREEN

Everything he taps with his famous thumb turns green. The north side of the tree, then the other three directions, the humpbacked boulder, the bottom foot of the white stucco wall, the wooden shingles. You'd swear the cedar deck was the surface of a legless snooker table covered in felt. Moss grows on the back of the sloth that hasn't moved for days from its hammock in the trees. In his presence, berries and fruit of all kinds never ripen, except gooseberries, except kiwis and limes. You see him in the gaze of the jade-eyed cat. When he looks at you, the glint of fallen snow kindles the green receptors in your retinas, the sea turns phosphorescent, and fireflies, hovering above the hedges like levitating emerald chips, catch in the hairs on your arms, in your eyebrows, in your shy moustache.

God of INDIFFERENCE

You suspect you made this one up.

It makes the sound of silkworms, soft, soft.

Looking for it is like looking for the drugged.

So what? Who cares? Who knows?

It's all relative, it's all context.

He slammed the door so hard the window

broke. Taped cardboard over it

and it stayed like that your whole childhood.

Who cares? Blessed are the cool.

The empty. Pick a number. Any one.

God of THE SELF-DEFEATING

Nostrils bully the taste buds; savory routs what's sweet, the mouth mistaking plums for lumps of Marmite. Sleep opposes the comfort of the goose down bed. The big toe disdains the little toe though they inhabit the same shoe. How dumb is that? When this god's in charge, greasy spoons at 6 a.m. get rid of coffee and stubbornly insist on pomegranate juice. In mid-July, winter for no good reason decides to occupy the summer house. Snow drifts through the screens onto the adulterers lying on the wicker couch, their sweat freezing into fragile quills along their fickle bellies, their marmoreal inner thighs. Yes says no to the loyal dog, the kind boss, the clean washing on the line. No to the driver who stops to pick you up on the remotest road in Saskatchewan. As the car disappears, a dust devil twists toward you from the emptiness ahead; you walk into its grit with open arms though you've just had your only bath in days.

FALSE GODS

These are the ones who show up at the party, grains of rapture bagged and tucked up their sleeves, heaven's golden mead in flasks in their secret pockets. They're everyone's best nightmare. They sit in the front of the club, stuff the biggest notes in the G-strings of the strippers. At the gym they work out beside the bouncer, lift so much weight they bless him with ambition until he has to turn his body sideways to walk through doorways and down the aisles of buses. You see yourself in the otherworldly shine of their briefcases, in their clever suits of mirrors. You never catch the colour of their eyes. Though clouds bust open, the false ones drive with the cloth tops down and don't get wet. They walk on swimming pools, holding aloft cocktails as pale as ichor. They watch over you with the patience of Styrofoam. What's your want? they whisper. Only one word is necessary to call them close—
need, need, need.

God of SNOW

During the longest nights she lets fall millions of stars, covering all, covering all, the ugly and the beautiful, the humble and the vain, and everything is hallowed in her eyes. Boughs of conifers grow heavy with their faith in this god's chaste intentions. Mice scrawl their journeys beneath the Milky Way; they tunnel in like arctic bookworms and live inside crystal tomes of snow. Tall blades of yellow grass trace empty circles across the surface of the drifts—a winter sense of time. When you walk in wonder your past fills in and disappears; your mind turns white, immaculate. You may be lost but you don't care. *No other gods,* you say as you break a trail across the frozen lake, breath frosting your scarf and lashes. What touches touches lightly and does not stay.

God of PUBLIC WASHROOMS

You see her sometimes in the face of the woman who pushes the bucket on wheels with its mop, its slosh of water, its bottles of cleaning fluids and rags. When your eyes meet in the bank of mirrors, something sparks and flutters in your breast like a siskin set on fire. This is a rare encounter. Usually you don't look at her. You're embarrassed by the tasks she executes in the row of cubicles high and narrow as confessionals. Her head is lowered, she has work to do. Sometimes you see this god when she squats on a stool by the entrance, in her lap a collection basket. For your coins you get a folded square of paper you never read. The toilet flush is a water-logged bell that summons her inside. You wish you'd used the stall to release a paper bag of yellow butterflies, to leave on top of the tank a swaddled Bethlehem baby; at the very least, to write on the metal door the verse of a psalm that will convince her of your specialness, your lyrical devotion, as she scrubs all natural signs of you away.

God of NEVER

Poe got it right. This god's familiar is her raven. Her celestial omen, the Dark Moon. Really, what we call "the first lunar phase" is no moon at all. Once a month, raven plucks the silver disc from the sky and tucks it in a clamshell to show earthlings what a never-moon could mean. This god's around if you've never kissed a fool, never stitched a wound, never given up on searching for a theory that explains your life. She's there when you understand happily never after. Never say never, the self-help books advise. Beware the never-dog who's never found a home. Imagine never being done. Never being broken. Never living in a body loved so much the soul is loath to leave.

God of THE GAPS

The god of sex, the god of insects—both claim they're the busiest but the god of the gaps doesn't get a coffee break, a day off, a Sunday-morning snooze: this is the god invented to explain what science can't. Think of the disparities, rifts, lacunae, that baffle PhDs; add to that the other mysteries she must watch over. Let's consider just one—the workings of the human heart. Cardiologists have plotted its dimensions, diseases, function, but they are dumb when it comes to its devotions, to its propensity to break. Einstein, who walked in wonder, quipped, "You can't blame gravity for falling in love." Though it won't do you any good, you *can* blame the god of the gaps.

God of SLOUGHS

You can tell he's a western god or he'd be called the god of ponds. Sloughs are not romantic. You can't imagine someone serenading offshore, tossing petals in the wake. One out of ten on the prairies is alkali, white crusting around the edges. He got the idea from the god of frost though alkali to its advantage survives the heat. You can't drink from a slough, but ducks paddle in the reeds, the eggs of red-winged black-birds balance in the swaying bulrushes, and the sky falls into it as it would into nicer water, clouds stiffening and flattening like starched handkerchiefs a laundress from long ago hangs out to dry.

God of PAIN

On a scale of 1 to 10, how bad is it? How are you to know? Is 10 a decapitation or a hornet sting? Is 3 a penis rubbing the atrophied walls of an old vagina? Does the 3 drop to 1 if the woman comes? This god is the loneliest. No one wants him. You stand corrected—he created masochists, after all. At the festivals a hundred or so of the worst of them turn up to carry his effigies from cemetery to chapel. Sometimes he takes the form of a horse's bowel tied in a knot, other times ripped rotator cuffs shown on X-rays carried like stiff flags on poles. There are clinics in his name. Big pharmaceuticals get rich. People plead with him to shift the suffering of their beloved to them. He won't do it. What you own you own, he tells them; that's true for pain more than any other thing. Finally agony is all that's left, no matter who you were before it started, what good you did. This divinity moulds a new you out of burns and aches and shattering, and leaves you with it. He watches over, yes, you bet, but his eyes are cold.

God of OWLS

You want there to be a separate god for owls, for the barred, the burrowing, the saw-whet, the spotted, the great horned, the barn owl whose gaze draws you to his wide face and you see yourself, pale, uncanny. You want this god to keep these birds from harm so the night will be lavishly feathered. Their wings in flight will row through the waters of your sleep and you'll sense the dip and rise of them, the sky riddled with eyes. You want this god to instruct them not to scoop a cat into the sky, or a family's only chicken. You want the slow unrolling of the owls' vowels to slip into your speaking. So much, so little they have to say. You want the owls' silence to be this god's silence, one that doesn't mean there's no one there, but a refined and honed attention, a keen listening high above you, and a steady looking down.

EPILOGUE: I KNOW YOUR WORKS

I am the first and the last.

I am the cat and the crocodile,

the manta ray and the nostrils of the newt.

I am the nipple and the hard heel of the foot.

I am the spoil that swells the belly, I am

the stone's spasm and the death cry

of the barley field. Look for me

in the bowels of the rhinoceros,

in the hollow bones of the listing hawk.

In song, in not-song you will find me.

I am your birth and your never-waking,

your lungs sinking into clay. I am

their anguished breath, their weight

of mossy stones. I know your works.

I was there when you were fashioned

from tar and ruin and pity,

all your eyes becoming two eyes,

your hundred weary hearts

compressing into one.

The quotation italicized in "God of Sex" is attributed to Leonardo da Vinci. Found in *Bluets,* Maggie Nelson (Wave Books, 2009) p. 23. *Lawn dolphins* in "God of Renaming" is a term invented by poets Jim Bertolino and Anita K. Boyle in their attempt to rehabilitate slugs. The quotation that ends "God of the Mutable" is the traditional Ashanti way of beginning to tell a tale.

The sources of the epigraphs at the beginning of the book and in each section are as follows: Pessoa, from "A Factless Autobiography," *The Book of Disquiet* (ed. & trans. Richard Zenith, Penguin, 2003) p. 26; Mirabi, from *The Soul Is Here For Its Own Joy* (ed. Robert Bly, Ecco, 1999) p. 191; Roberto Calasso, from *Literature and the Gods* (trans. Tim Parks, Knopf, 2001) p. 3; Emily Dickinson, from one of her letters (from a book I have misplaced); Stephen Dunn, from "Dostoyevsky in Wildwood" in *Local Visitations* (W.W. Norton & Co., 2003) p. 90; Paul Verlaine, from "Les Dieux," as quoted in Calasso on p. 19.

Earlier versions of some of these poems appeared in *The Malahat Review, The Harlequin,* and *In/Words.* Several were featured in *The Philosophical Salon* of the *Los Angeles Review of Books.*

My thanks go to my publisher, especially Jared Bland, Anita Chong, Kelly Joseph, Jen Lum (the wonderful designer), and Heather Sangster, (my sharp-eyed copy-editor). Special thanks to Donna Bennett for her friendship and support, and her wit and wisdom as my editor. She's been with me since 1985. I also want to thank Patrick Lane, who helps me find the holy in every day.

LORNA CROZIER is the author of sixteen previous books of poetry, including *What the Soul Doesn't Want*, *The Wrong Cat*, *Small Mechanics*, *The Blue Hour of the Day: Selected Poems*, and *Whetstone*. She is also the author of *The Book of Marvels: A Compendium of Everyday Things* and the memoir *Small Beneath the Sky*. She won the Governor General's Literary Award for Poetry for *Inventing the Hawk* and three additional collections were finalists for this prize. She has received the Canadian Authors Association Award, three Pat Lowther Memorial Awards, and the Dorothy Livesay Poetry Prize. She is a Professor Emerita at the University of Victoria and an Officer of the Order of Canada, and she has received five honorary doctorates for her contributions to Canadian Literature. She lives in British Columbia with writer Patrick Lane and two fine cats who love to garden.